ISBN-13 978-0984052714
ISBN-10 0984052712
Printed in United States of America

Published by Threshold Therapeutics Media
Natick, Ma
www.thresholdtherapeuticsmedia.com

Breathe

It's me...

Kali.

I have

questions for

you.

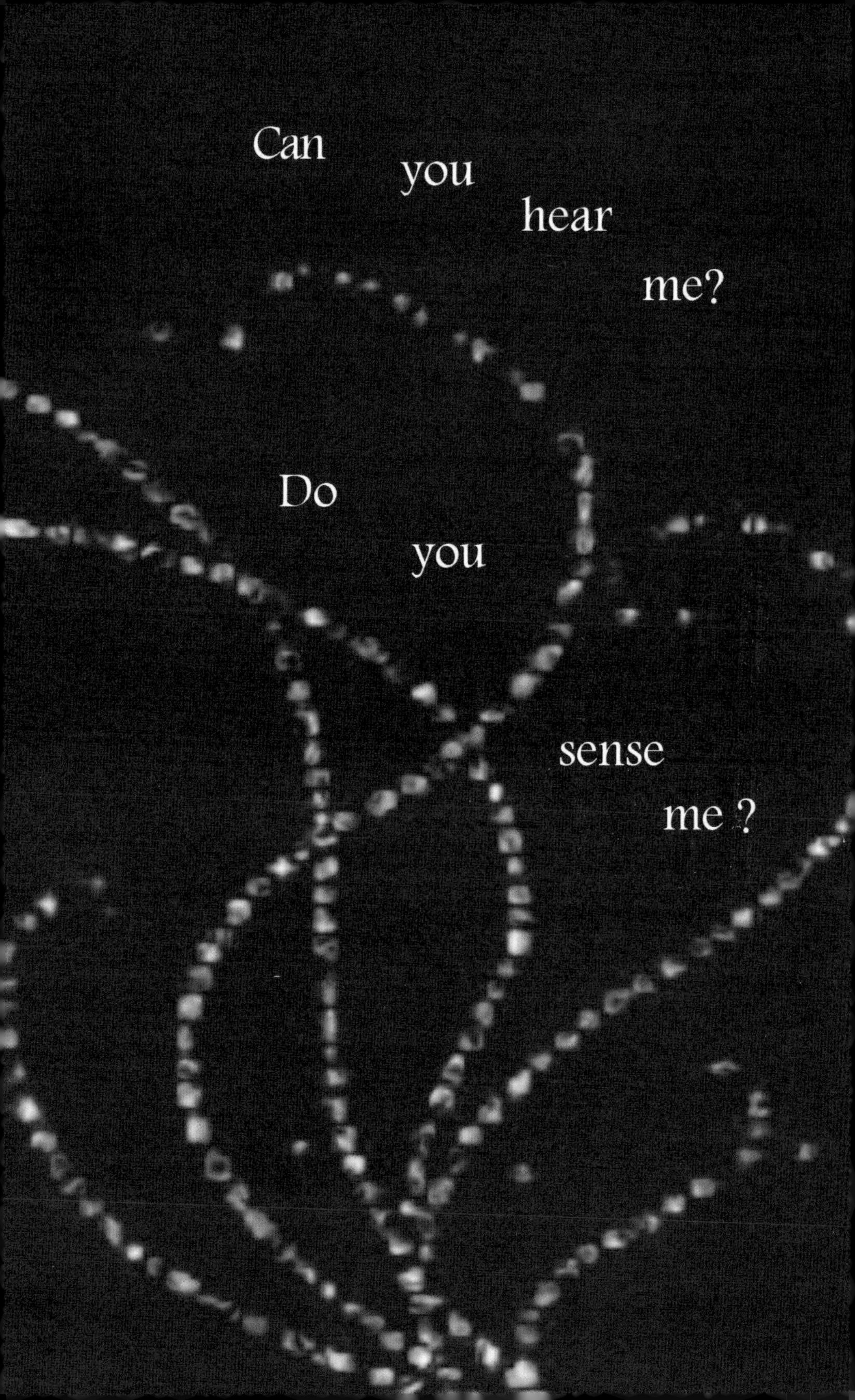

Can
you
hear
me?

Do
you
sense
me ?

I am here to clear the way.

I personify those stirrings and

forces in your psyche

that seem like death to you

but which I reveal

to be a vital part

of the process needed to

transform

your

life.

You imagine

DEATH

to be

AGONY

... to be

THE END.

You do not
recognize

that labor pains

also begin.

I am the undertaker and the midwife

at the point in the cycle where

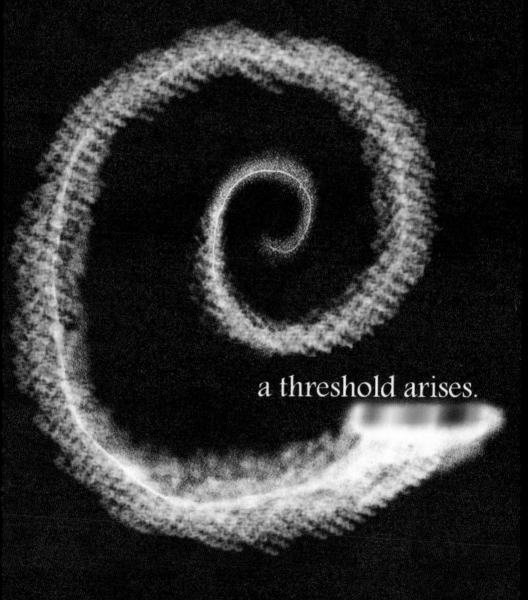

a threshold arises.

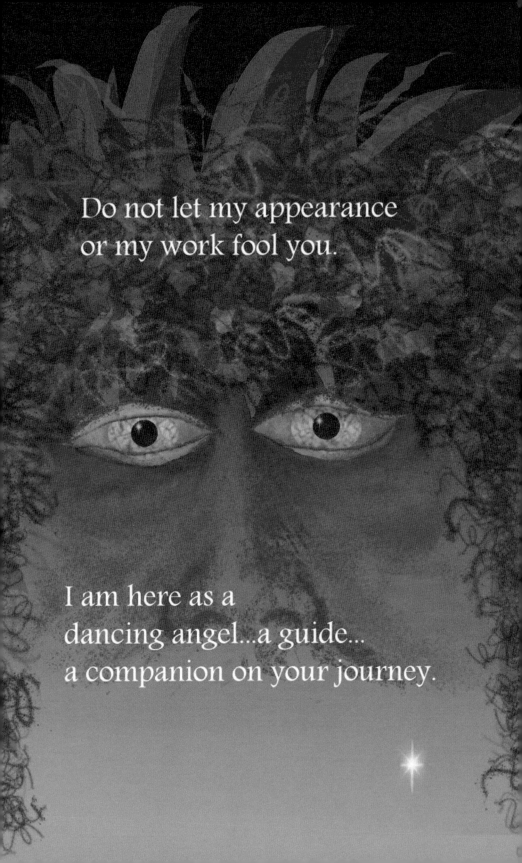

Do not let my appearance
or my work fool you.

I am here as a
dancing angel...a guide...
a companion on your journey.

I want to help you reawaken
the knowledge you hold
in your heart and soul,
the knowledge deep within your cells,

the knowledge of cycles...

cycles of creation
and destruction,
rebirth and death,
summer and winter,
day and night,
high tides and low,
full moons and new,
the in breath
and the out,

the out breath
and the in,
new moons and full,
low tides and high,
night and day,
winter and summer,
death and rebirth,
cycles of destruction
and creation.

I am here
to remind you
that out of death,
a seeming void,
new is born...

that destruction
and grief are
creative.
They help
birth

new ways.

So,
What must die ?

The fear
that after death
there is only emptiness.
The fear
that change
means outer horror.

Instead, dear one,
consider that the
essential
change
is
INSIDE.

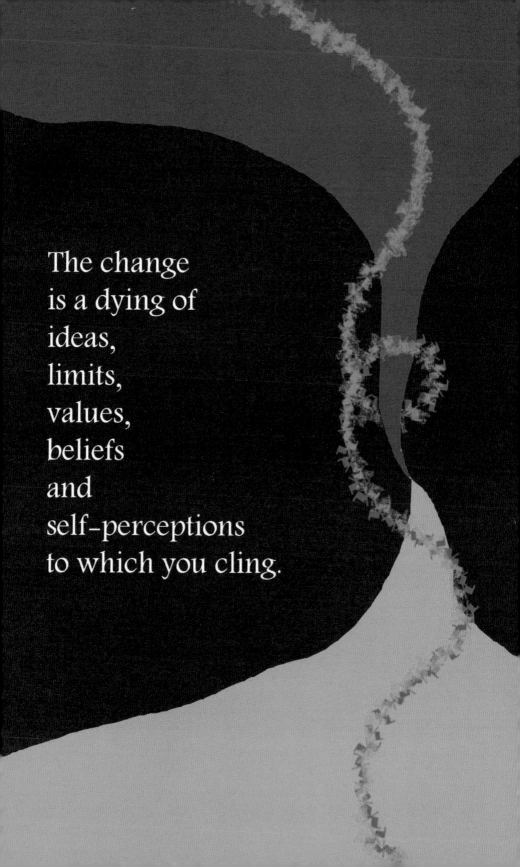

The change
is a dying of
ideas,
limits,
values,
beliefs
and
self-perceptions
to which you cling.

So, I ask

what must die?

What must die?

What must die?

What must die?

what MUST die?

what must die?

See my moon tool?

It is sharp and gentle.

With it I can cut and cradle.

I hold the moon with the

power of the wave

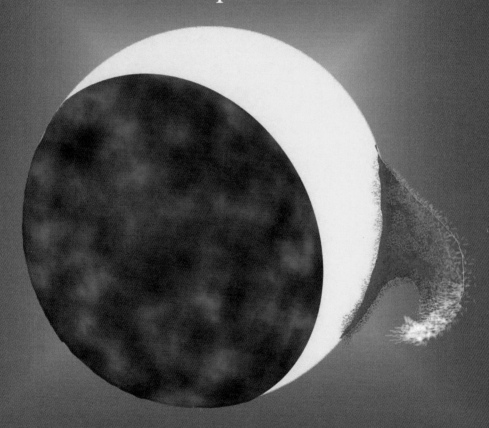

...symbols of the ever-present
movement that is Life.

I use
my tool
to cut away
thoughts
that strangle
and choke
emerging
Truths.

Fresh,
more
expansive
life awaits.

I am a loving companion,
   but I am also a strong taskmaster,
   demanding and often relentless.

I am so filled with love for you,
   that I crave to destroy anything
   in your inner world,
   anything that gets in your way.

I yearn for you to
   step through the threshold
   and birth yourself yet again.

I clear the way.

I release the old
so there is

truly room
for this tender beginning.

Then I rock all newness
in my moon tool,
the movement echoing the cycles.

As I rock, I plant seeds;
the seeds of strength,
                    courage,
                        wisdom
                            and
                                faith

                                to
                            carry
                        forth...

to meet me again in the future.

For
you will,

as you grow,
meet me every time

you need to
shed the old and

birth the new.

I plant too, a spark
that you may tend
and stoke into a fire
that burns with life-giving
passion of the
Truths you know so deep.

The choice to tend the flame is yours.

But should the world
come close to
extinguishing
your flames,

you will,

in your soul,

cry for me.

And I will come.

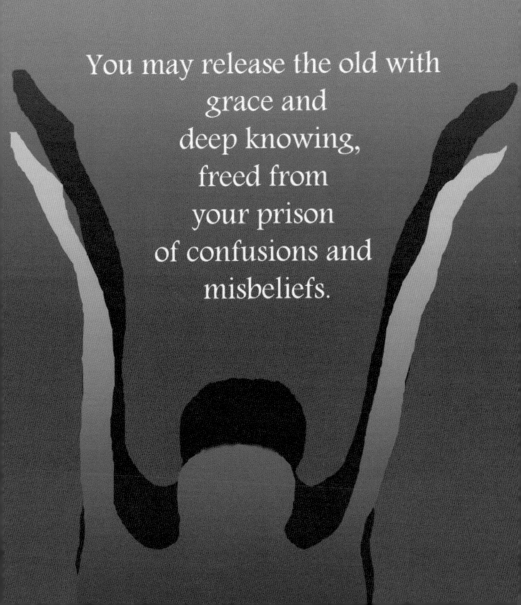

You may greet me with
open arms and heart,
surrendering easily
to the kiss of
my moon tool.

You may release the old with
grace and
deep knowing,
freed from
your prison
of confusions and
misbeliefs.

OR,
if you have ingested the ideas
you are offered every day,
the fears taught
in your world,
we will battle.

If you believe

that my way is horrid,
that death chants,
endings, bones and
even seeds are empty,
that I am to be avoided...

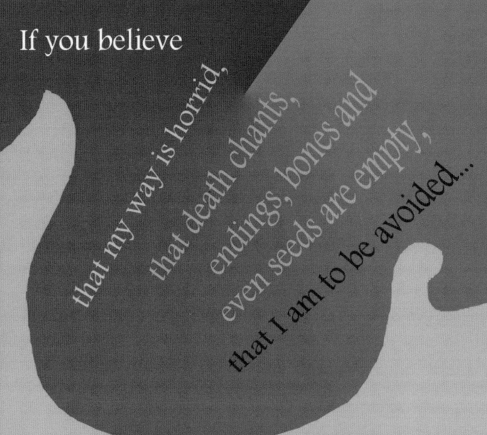

...if you have absorbed the lies,

when you see me,

you will cower and

try to hide.

You may shriek
"NO!"
and cling tightly to what
you see as protection!

Protection ?

You ARE confused!

I do not seek to harm you...

I am
here to free
you!

I will be deeply saddened
by any struggle,
for you will
lose so much more if
you fight.

It is the
Way of Nature.

Resist me not,
and my work will be
to gently prune the
branches that wither,
the vines that strangle.

You may

sense relief

and

feel gratitude.

Sometimes,
even if you do not oppose me
you may grieve.

Do what you must
to keep your heart
truly open,
for a
closed heart
is like
a blocked
birth canal.

If you resist,
if you do not,

if you weep
or welcome,

if you wail
or rest,

I fully witness you
and fill your cup with hope
until you arrive at the threshold
and step through once again.

Trust me. I accompany you.
I rock you,
plant seeds and sparks
and send you
on your way
to a higher turn
in the ever expanding
spiral
that
is
Life.

Don't you see ?

You return to me again

and again.

I love you

and I bless you.

And I hold you with song,

so you remember.

Yes, I do all Life's bidding

while singing

infinite melodies

to awaken you.

Embody the tones,

the sounds.

feel the songs with your tongue,
taste the notes with your nose,
smell the chords with your ears,
see the tunes with your skin,
hear the harmonies with your eyes,

and...

allow the

music

to

move

your body.

Allow yourself to

feel

your soul!

I dance

destruction and birth.

They are not opposites or tensions.
They are sounds in the

Song of Life!

And I love to sing!

I sing you into death,
    while severing the old.

       I sing you through grief,
       offering harmonies
       to soothe you.

       I sing you into the spaces

       between

    the out breath and the in.

I sing you to the threshold,
    knowing so much more awaits.

       I sing you into new life,
        my melodies carrying
         you forward.

All this,

while I sing too,

an undertone

of glory

for

your

journey.

It is magnificent!

Yes, dear one...simply feel!
Song is everywhere!

Songs of release,

songs of delight,

songs of uprising,

songs of clearing,

songs of receiving,

songs of integration,

songs of daring,

songs of connection...

Fear not the songs, for they are part of

All That Is–

all you understand all your experience

all you outgrow...death of old ways...

birth of new ways...your new life

all you understand...all you experience

all you outgrow...death of old ways

your ever expanding Eternal Essence.

birth of new ways...your new life

And the songs

are so beautiful...

and

so

are

YOU!

Rest

Do you still fear me ?

Have you not felt my love for you ?

Rest in the truth

    that if much

        becomes overgrown,

           I will gladly

               clear the way

                   so that TRULY

you can bloom

again

and

again

and

again....

You are perennial!

Now, I invite you to

take a breath

pause

release that breath

You do not miss that old breath,
do you ?

What must die ?

What will be born ?

I am here.

Made in the USA
Charleston, SC
24 January 2015